Monographic Journals of the Near East *Syro-Mesopotamian Studies* 4/3 (December 1982)

THE DESCENT OF INANNA AS A RITUAL JOURNEY TO KUTHA?

by
Giorgio Buccellati

A CATALOG OF NEAR EASTERN VENUS DEITIES

by
Wolfgang Heimpel

Two complementary articles dealing with the Sumerian tale of Inanna's descent to the netherworld, with a survey of Near Eastern Venus deities. Buccellati proposes that the Inanna of the story was not only a divine person, but was, in addition, a statue on a ritual journey from southern to northern Babylonia (Kutha). Heimpel rediscovers that she was also, in addition to these two aspects, the planet Venus. One may wonder about this seemingly illogical concept, but the conclusion appears to be inescapable—that the Sumerians combined all three aspects in their belief about the same deity in the same tale.

Table of Contents

THE DESCENT OF INANNA AS A RITUAL JOURNEY TO KUTHA?

Giorgio Buccellati
University of California, Los Angeles

The Sumerian *Descent of Inanna*[1] relates, in a poetic narrative form, events and situations of the divine world—it is, in the common understanding of the word, a myth. It seems, however, possible to suggest a cultic setting for the story, which, if correct, would improve our understanding of certain aspects of the text, would add immediacy and concreteness to its *Sitz im Leben* and might also help in dating the composition. There are two parts to my argument.

1. The Itinerary of Inanna's Journey

The first is geographical in nature. The beginning of the Sumerian version states that Inanna "abandoned" her various temples in a number of Sumerian cities and "descended" to the Netherworld. The cities are mentioned by name; in the order in which they are introduced in one manuscript,[2] they are Uruk, Badtibira, Zabalam, Adab, Nippur, Kish and Akkad. Checking their location on the map, one notices that the sequence corresponds to a line going from the south to the northwest,[3] except for an initial swing to the east from Uruk to Badtibira. The "abandoning" of her cities on the part of Inanna may then be taken not as a simultaneous happening, but as a progression of events: she abandons one city after another as she goes *from* one *to* the next in a generally northward direction. But where does this progression lead? The last city mentioned by name in the sequence is Akkad, yet we know that this is not the destination point, since at the very beginning of the story we are told that the goddess "sets her mind to the Great Below" and "descended to the Netherworld." Now, if we continue on the map in the same northerly direction as is indicated by the sequence of cities, a very natural destination point presents itself at the end of the line: Kutha. Kutha is the residence of the Netherworld gods, and in point of fact the Akkadian version of the myth refers explicitly to the Netherworld as Kutha: "Enter, my lady, that *Kutha* may rejoice over thee," says the gatekeeper to Ishtar when she is about to enter the Netherworld (Obv. 40).

[1] On this text see S. N. Kramer, "Inanna's Descent to the Nether World" Continued and Revised, *JCS* 5 (1951):1-17; Idem, Cuneiform Studies and the History of Literature: the Sumerian Sacred Marriage Texts, *PAPS* 107(1963):491-93, 510-16; A. Falkenstein, Der Sumerische und der Akkadische Mythos von Inannas Gang zur Unterwelt, *in* E. Graf (ed.), *Festschrift W. Caskel,* Leiden, 1968, 96-110; S. N. Kramer, *The Sacred Marriage Rite,* Bloomington, 1969, 107-121; T. Jacobsen, *The Treasures of Darkness,* New Haven and London, 1976, 55-61. I wish to thank Thorkild Jacobsen and Jerrold Cooper for their comments on an earlier version of the manuscript. [See also below, n. 14]

[2] Ni 368 & CBS 9800; other manuscripts present some variation in the sequence and/or the list of names.

[3] A similar geographical orientation is also to be found in other Mesopotamian texts, see the discussion by C. Wilcke, Der aktuelle Bezug der Sammlung der sumerischen Tempelhymnen und ein Fragment eines Klageliedes, *ZA* 62(1972):39-42.

Before plotting the course of Inanna's voyage on a map, two more observations are in place. First, the cities listed are at an even distance, approximately, one from the other (leaving aside Akkad, for which no firm localization can be advanced): this would be consistent with the notion of a journey which requires interruptions at intermediary stations regularly spaced one from the other. The second remark is that when Inanna is finally released from the Netherworld, she returns to Uruk by the same road, except that only two stations are explicitly mentioned in the preserved portion of the text, one of them (Umma) probably taking the place of another city in the same vicinity (Zabalam) mentioned in the north-bound journey, while the other (Badtibira) remains the same in both portions of the trip.

We may now transfer our remarks onto a map,[4] indicating the course of the ancient rivers and canals, the names of the cities listed in Inanna's itinerary and, in parentheses, the most important cities omitted in the same itinerary:

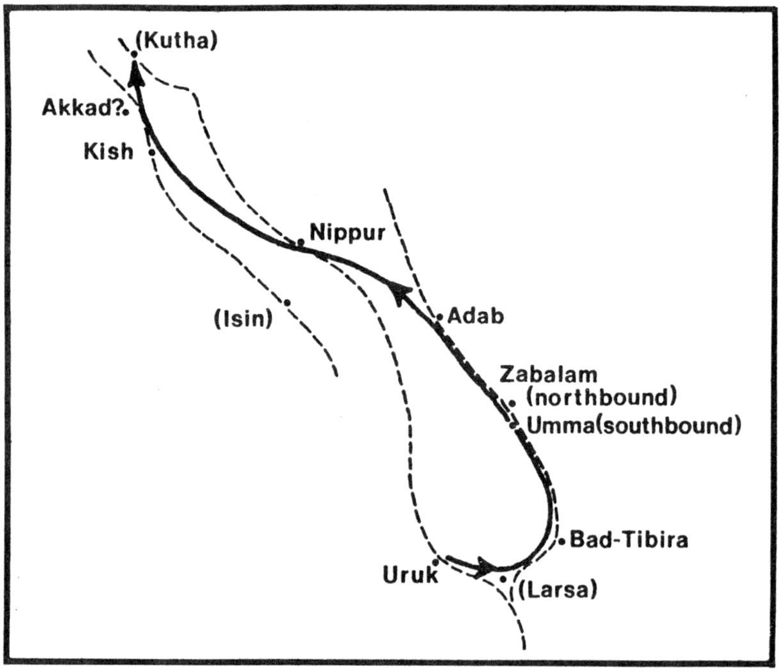

[4] Based on the surveys of Jacobsen and Adams, see T. Jacobsen, The Waters of Ur, *Iraq* 22(1960): 174-185, Pl. XXVIII = T. Jacobsen, *Toward the Image of Tammuz and Other Essays*, Cambridge, 1970, 230-243; R. M. Adams, Survey of Ancient Water Courses and Settlements in Central Iraq, *Sumer* 14(1958): 101-3, figs. 1-6; Th. Jacobsen, A Survey of the Girsu (Telloh) Region, *Sumer* 25(1969):103-109; R. McC. Adams and H. J. Nissen, *The Uruk Countryside: The Natural Setting of Urban Societies*, Chicago and London, 1972, 2-3 and 42-46.

The initial detour to the East, in the direction of Badtibira and then up to Zabalam, may be explained on the basis of the special connection between Inanna and those cities. But it is also tempting to suppose that the choice of the Eastern instead of the Western branch of the Euphrates was due to the need of bypassing Isin, which was the main city on the direct northbound route from Uruk. If so (and the highly tentative nature of this hypothesis should be stressed) one may venture to suggest further that the text was composed geographically within the sphere of influence of Larsa, and chronologically at a time when Isin had begun to lose its political importance and territorial control, but was still in control of the main canal route between Uruk and Nippur.

2. Does the Myth Refer to the Cultic Renewal of a Statue?

A second line of reasoning which corroborates the argumentation advanced so far pertains to the nature of Inanna as she appears in the text. Following a suggestion of a former student of mine, Dr. Paul Gaebelein, I would like to see in certain portions of the text a reference to a *statue* of the goddess. The pertinent passages are two. First, the description of Inanna given by her messenger to the supreme gods in an effort to stir their compassion and interest in the miserable plight of the goddess acquires a much greater poignancy if it is taken to refer to an actual statue:

> "O Father Enlil, let not your daughter be put to death in the Netherworld,
> Let not your good metal be covered with the dust of the Netherworld,
> Let not your good lapis lazuli be broken up into the stone of the stoneworker,
> Let not your boxwood be cut up into the wood of the woodworker. . ."[5]

Second, the well-known sequence during which Inanna is disrobed could be conceived in a literal sense, as referring to a cultic setting, whereby a statue would in fact be disrobed and then dressed once again.[6] This would presume the performing of a ritual which would enact physically on a statue what the myth describes through the narrative.[7]

I do not intend to suggest here that the text, as we now have it, should be interpreted as a cultic libretto which would have accompanied the ritual action. The myth is essentially narrative, and the underlying plot cannot be understood simply in terms of an unfolding ritual. My interpretation would only presuppose that *some aspects* of the narrative were inspired by a ritual and can still be analyzed as such even though they were transposed

[5] Ll. 43-46, in the translation of Kramer, *Sacred Marriage Rite,* quoted, p. 108. Note, however, the different interpretation of this passage by Jacobsen, *Treasures,* quoted, p. 57, where an indicative, instead of an imperative, is implied: if Enlil does not let his silver, precious stones or hardwood be damaged, how could he let his own daughter Inanna be harmed?

[6] On the use of garments for divine statues see A. L. Oppenheim, The Golden Garments of the Gods, *JNES* 8 (1949), especially pp. 179f.; W. F. Leemans, *Ishtar of Lagaba and Her Dress,* Leiden, 1952, 19-24.

[7] On the possible connection between statues and another type of text, the hymns to deities, see W. W. Hallo, The Cultic Setting of Sumerian Poetry, *RAI* 17, Bruxelles, 1970, 119. For the performance dimension of ritual see T. Jacobsen, Religious Drama in Ancient Mesopotamia, *in* H. Goedicke and J. J. M. Roberts (eds.), *Unity and Diversity,* Baltimore and London, 1975, 65-97; for the role of statues in ritual see *ibid.*, pp. 71, 73.

within the framework of a true narrative myth. (The myth itself may in turn have been used as part of a festival,[8] but that of course is a different question.) The narrative myth as such is *not* to be understood as a liturgy *tout court*, and so some of its aspects appear to pose a problem for a simple cultic interpretation. For example, it is difficult to envisage exactly just what is meant by the fact that Inanna is said to "leave" the various sanctuaries which, in my interpretation, serve as stations on a processional way: was it one and the same statue touching down at the various stations and then setting off again, or were different statues joining the procession at each different sanctuary? And how about the return—was it also ceremonial, and if so how are we to account for the developments in the action which involve Inanna's entourage, especially Dumuzi? These problems may well remain insoluble from the viewpoint of a cultic interpretation, and may have to be explained only in terms of the myth. But even if the contribution of a cultic interpretation remains fragmentary, it seems nevertheless valid within given limitations and useful in throwing new light on certain aspects of the text.

Within these limitations, we may conjecture further on a possible *Sitz im Leben* for the assumed ritual. This may have been an annual renewal ceremony, which may have been a part of the regular, recurrent caring of the goddess, and might have originated in response to the breaking of a given statue, whether accidental or through enemy intervention.[9] A broken statue would explain the emphasis in the passage just quoted on the material components of the object: metal, stone and wood are reduced to raw materials once the unity of the anthropomorphic character has been lost. If the destruction of the statue was understood as the (temporary) dying of the deity, and if the dead deity was conceived as having gone to the Netherworld, then the journey to Kutha was a symbolic action through which one was retracing the steps of the dead goddess to her temporary location. There may have been, in other words, a ritual procession[10] during which the concrete counterpart of the dead goddess (i.e., the broken statue) was brought to Kutha, as if only there, where the dead goddess "really" was, could the broken statue be restored to its integrity—for to restore a broken divine statue is more than a simple act of craftsmanship, it is a religious act surrounded by

[8] Cf. H. Sauren, Besuchsfahrten der Götter in Sumer, *Or* NS 38(1969):232f.

[9] The almost complete lack in the archaeological finds of monumental divine statues is sometimes explained through the hypothesis of enemy plundering, see A. Spycket, *Les statues de culte dans les textes Mésopotamiens des origines à la Ire dynastie de Babylone,* Paris, 1968, 11 (the author does not consider our text in her documentation). A ritual text from Seleucid times speaks about the accidental breaking of a royal statue, *op. cit.,* p. 90. See also L. Cagni, *The Poem of Erra, SANE* 1/3, Malibu, 1977, 32f., 1.133 with n. 36.

[10] The procession was a common institution of Babylonian religion as was the mythical account of divine journeys from one city to another, see among others B. Meissner, *Babylonien und Assyrien,* 1(1920): 293; 2(1925):63, 92, 101, 126, 169ff.; A. Salonen, Prozessionswagen der babylonischen Götter, *St. Or.* 13/2(1946):3; N. Schneider, Götterschiffe im Ur III-Reich, *St. Or.* 13/5(1946):7, 10ff.; H. Sauren, Besuchsfahrten des Götter in Sumer, *Or* NS 38(1969):214-36; A. Sjöberg, Götterreisen, *RLA* III/6-7(1969): 480-82; Hallo, Cultic Setting, quoted, p. 120; D. Reisman, Ninurta's Journey to Eridu, *JCS* 24(1971):3-10; A. J. Ferrara, *Nanna-Suen's Journey to Nippur, Studia Pohl* SM2, Rome, 1973; B. Alster, On the Interpretation of the Sumerian Myth "Inanna and Enki," *ZA* 64(1975):20-34, especially 28f.; Jacobsen, Religious Drama, quoted, p. 67.

religious symbolism.[11] The symbolism which would characterize this particular ceremony is quite complex and the requirements made on the human community (a long processional journey) rather demanding. But even a trip across the land of Sumer[12] simply to perform the ritual renewal of a statue may not seem exaggerate, particularly if one considers two other aspects of the situation. On the one hand, the politics of territorial expansion pursued by the Larsa kings (if I am correct in dating the text to just this time) would welcome any opportunity to assert the unity of the territories then being brought under their control–and a procession arching its way around Isin from south to north would serve very well this purpose. On the other hand, the use of divine statues seems to have become more common precisely with the Old Babylonian period,[13] which may imply that at that time the role of the statue in the cult was still being defined, thus leaving ample room for creative innovation and experimentation, even of a type which was not going to be taken up and continued in the later periods of Mesopotamian religion.[14]

[11] Note in this connection the suggestion by Y. Rosengarten, Au sujet d'un théâtre religieux sumérien, *RHR* 174(1968):122, that the lamentation over the destruction of Ur was part of a liturgy commemorating the destruction of the city and possibly the return to it of its main goddess, Ningal; but cf. also Hallo, Cultic Setting, quoted, p. 119.

[12] Long journeys are not unusual for divine processions, cf. Sauren, Besuchsfahrten, quoted, p. 234.

[13] See Spycket, *Statues de culte*, quoted, p. 99.

[14] A recent book about the myth is S. B. Perera, *Descent to the Goddess: A Way of Initiation for Women*, "Studies in Jungian Psychology, 6," Toronto: Inner City Books, 1981. Written from the viewpoint of Jungian psychology, rather than Assyriology, it offers little in the way of an exegesis to the myth; it is, however, interesting as a committed re-reading of an ancient text in the light of contemporary concerns–to the point of establishing a quasi-religious empathy with the protagonists of the myth. Nothing in the book has a direct bearing on the interpretation proposed in this article.

Another recent non-Assyriological book deals at some length with the Descent of Inanna–W. I. Thompson, *The Time Falling Bodies Take to Light: Mythology, Sexuality and the Origins of Culture*, New York: St. Martin's Press, 1981, pp. 172-181. Besides a psychological interpretation similar to that proposed by Perera ("descent into the subconscious"), there is special emphasis on an astral interpretation based on the movements of Venus and Mercury (= Enki, p. 174) around the Winter Solstice. This, too, however, has no bearing on the interpretation proposed in my article.

In a paper entitled "Observations on a Passage in 'Inanna's Descent' " presented at the 29th Rencontre Assyriologique Internationale held in London in July 1982 while this article was in press, A. George has suggested a similar interpretation of ll. 43-46 as referring to a statue.

A Catalog of Near Eastern Venus Deities

Wolfgang Heimpel
The University of California, Berkeley

Astral interpretation of ancient Mesopotamian narrative texts was overused in the early years of Assyriology. It discredited itself when it became apparent that these texts could not be explained as metaphoric expression of stars and planets alone. One consequently kept away from this particular avenue of interpretation, an attitude which has not much changed until now, and was shared by myself. As a result of conversations with B. Alster on this subject, it occurred to me that I knew of two cases where only an astral interpretation elucidated a text passage. The first case is the coincidence of the missing rear of the zodiac sign Taurus with that part of the Akkadian Gilgamesh epic where Enkidu throws a hindleg of the Bull of Heaven in Ishatar's face.[1] The second case is Inanna's answer to the question of the gatekeeper of the netherworld in which she identified herself as "Inanna towards sunrise."[2] In pursuing the planetary aspect of Inanna, I felt the need for a summary of our knowledge about Near Eastern Venus deities in general. This is provided here in the form of a catalogue. It turns out that they are all interrelated, yet derive from two different roots: a female Sumerian Venus deity and a male Semitic one.

1. Inanna

On the way to accomplish her bold plan to take over the rule of the netherworld from her sister, Ereshkigal, Inanna encounters her first obstacle in the person of Neti, the gatekeeper

[1] Cf. Gössmann *Planetarium Babylonicum* no. 77.

[2] "Already stated in a general way by Thureau-Dangin, *RA* 11 (1915) 141. After completion of this manuscript, Timothy Seymour of UCLA informed me of an article by H. C. Hostetter (A Planetary Visit to Hades, *Bulletin of the Center for Archaeoastronomy* II/4 [1979] 7ff.) which provides a planetary interpretation of the tale as a whole. The author sees in Inanna's descent to the netherworld, and her way through the gates of its palace, the planet Venus setting in the morning sky. As the planet gets closer to the horizon it loses in luminescence, a process which he likens to Inanna's passing through the gates. She is killed by the time the planet is not any more visible. The now following movements of Ninshubur are likened to the movements of Mercury. Her stay in Ur is seen as Mercury in the eastern sky, her stay in Nippur as Mercury in the western sky. Inanna is alive again when she appears in the evening sky, passing through the gates again in the opposite direction, which means that she gains luminescence.

As I shall demonstrate, the tale has Inanna moving from the western evening sky to the eastern morning sky, and not vice versa, as Kramer's translation seems to have been understood by Hostetter. Further, in the abundant cuneiform literature dealing with stars and planets, neither the gates of the palace of the netherworld, nor Ninshubar are mentioned. We have to conclude that the gates were believed to be located beneath the horizon at all times, and that Ninshubur was not Mercury.

I wish to express my gratitude to G. Azarpay for a number of references concerning the goddess Nanay; and to S. Alwaya for assistance in matters of Arabic sources.

of the netherworld. In the Akkadian version of the tale as she overcomes it by threat of physical force; in the Sumerian version, by deceit. The pertinent passage is contained in lines 72-87 of S.N. Kramer's edition, whose translation is quoted here with minor modifications:[3]

> "When Inanna had come near to the palace Lapismountain,
> she acted evilly at the door to the netherworld,
> she spoke evilly at the main gate of the netherworld.
> 'Open up the house, gatekeeper, open up the house,
> open up the house, Neti, open up the house. Somebody is here.
> Let me enter.'
> Neti, the chief gatekeeper of the netherworld,
> answers pure Inanna:
> 'Who are you?'
> 'I am Inanna towards the place where Utu rises.'[4]
> 'If you are Inanna towards the place where Utu rises,
> why do you go to the land of no return,
> why do you take the road whose traveller returns not?'
> Pure Inanna answers him:
> 'To witness the funeral rites
> of my elder sister Ereshkigal's
> husband, the lord Gugalana, who has died.'"

Inanna could have identified herself by giving just her name. By adding her destination, she wants to dispel the suspicions of the gatekeeper. She claims to be on her way to the eastern sky, which gives her the opportunity to pay her condolences to her sister. We do not know the catch of the second answer, but we can easily understand that of the first. She refers to herself as the planet Venus on the way from the western evening sky to the eastern morning sky. In modern terminology, this journey is known as inferior conjunction. It is a time when the planet is invisible for about one week. For the Sumerians, the planet, that is, the goddess Inanna, travelled during this time from west to east beneath the horizon where they also located the netherworld. Its gatekeeper must have seen Inanna crossing in the distance, westward or eastward, at times.

It is, of course, a well-known fact that Inanna was identified with the planet Venus. Astronomical and astrological texts provide clear identifications. In recordings of Venus positions from the eighth year of Ammisaduqa (1639)[5] the planet is called Ninsi'ana, a name of Inanna which already appears in an inscription of Amar-Su'en (2046-2038)[6] and the hymn

[3] *JCS* 5 (1951) 4ff.

[4] Kramer's translation "I am Inanna of the place where Utu rises" does not render the terminative case. Jacobsen already translates "towards" in *Treasures of Darkness*, page 56. With his translation, the ground for an astral interpretation is laid. "To the place . . . " is actually an elliptical expression for "on the way to the place . . . " as, for example in Gudea, Cyl. A II 5 uru-ni sirara ^{ki}-šè i_7-sirara^{ki}-du-a má mu-ni-ri, "On the way to her city Sirara he steered the boat on the Sirara-bound canal." Edzard mentions the passage as illustration of the planetary aspect of Inanna in *WM* 85f., but adopts the translation of Kramer.

[5] Most recent edition, E. Reiner, *Bibliotheca Mesopotamica* II/1 (1975).

[6] *SAK* 200 h.

of Iddin-Dagan (1974-54)[7] which describes the celebration of the sacred marriage of that ruler with the goddess. This hymn is designated in the colophon as "herosong of Ninsi-'ana" and speaks of Inanna in the evening sky.[8] In the Old Babylonian starlist, Venus is designated as "star Ninsi'ana."[9] The name itself may refer to the planet.[10] If it is translated "Red lady of heaven" it may refer to the redness of the evening sky or morning sky over the western or eastern horizon where Venus is typically found. In the same hymn, Inanna is also called "star Dilbad" which is the most common designation of the planet in astronomical and astrological texts of the first millennium B.C. In that literature, the planet is also designated with the name Ishtar, the Akkadian Venus deity and counterpart of Inanna.

The relevance of the fact that Venus was identified with one single deity in Babylonia is evident if we contrast it with the beliefs concerning the planet among the ancient Greeks. The Greeks did not originally possess a Venus deity. Instead, they had two separate deities identified with the evening star and the morning star, Hesperos and Phosphoros or Heosphoros. Parmenides, or Pythagoras, realized around 500 B.C. that the morning star and the evening star were, in fact, one single planet. A little later, Aristotle called it the "star of Aphrodite." Originally, the goddess Aphrodite had nothing to do with the planet. The link was in all probability made as a result of Babylonian influence in the field of astronomy.[11] Parmenides, or Pythagoras, probably discovered the identity of the evening star with the morning star on their own, for they were free of mythological concepts, and led rather by observation and reasoning. They did not believe in Hesperos and Phosphoros. The Babylonians, on the other hand, could not have had such intellectual freedom. In Babylonia, the recognition of the identity of the evening star with the morning star must have preceded the link with a deity. Otherwise, one would expect to find a morning star deity and an evening star deity, just as in Greece. There is no trace of such deities in the earliest Babylonian, that is, the Sumerian pantheon. When and how the link between the planet and Inanna was made cannot be ascertained. It is prehistorical. As shall be seen, it was already complete when Inanna met Ishtar.

If one takes the liberty to speculate about manner and time of the link between the goddess and the planet, one has to ask, first, whether Inanna is a deification of the planet, just as Utu is the deification of the sun, and Nanna the deification of the moon; or second, whether Inanna existed as a deity before she was identified with the planet. If one subscribes to the theory that Sumerian gods, and gods of other polytheistic religions, grew out of man's awe of the powers of nature, the deification of the sun and the moon is understandable. They are obviously powers of nature with their clear impact on human life and life in general. In addition, the sun and the moon are most clearly defined in their individuality. They must have been prime objects of the process of deification of natural powers, and can be found as a result among all polytheistic religions. Planets like Venus and Jupiter may be a spectacle

[7] W.H. Ph. Roemer, *SKIZ*, chapter VI; D. Reisman, *JCS* 25 (1973) 185ff.

[8] T. Jacobsen understands lines 136ff. of this hymn as description of a morning scene (*Treasures of Darkness*, 138). I understand it as a variation on the description of the evening scene, lines 90ff.

[9] *MSL* XI 108, 394; cf. also *CT* 42, 6 III 18.

[10] It is written, ^{d}nin-si$_{4}$-an-na, ^{d}nin-si-an-na, and ^{d}nin-an-si$_{4}$-an-na.

[11] *RE* s.v. Planeten, 2031f. and 2113f.

for the eyes, yet as forces of nature they have little impact on man's life. One can do without them. Why were they deified at all? The reason for this probably lies in their movement, which sets them apart from the numberless stars they resemble, and likens them to the sun and the moon in whose path they move. The sun and the moon were gods, their movement, therefore, a divine quality. Were the planets then identified with pre-existing deities, or were they formed into deities by adding other, principally anthropomorphic, aspects? There are indications that the latter is the case. One of the designations of Jupiter in texts from the 1st millennium B.C. is Shulpa'e.[12] This god already exhibits "astral" aspects in a Sumerian hymn from the Old Babylonian period.[13] Moreover, his very name seems to express just that: "The-brightly-appearing-youth." It is already attested in tablets from Fara from around 2500 B.C. If this is the original name of the deity, his divinity derived from the recognition of the planet. The same may be true also of Marduk. He is identified with Jupiter and with Mercury in texts from the 1st millennium B.C.[14] Assuming that the link with Mercury is original, one can understand the name as derived from Amar-Utu, "Calf-of-the-sun."[15] Among the planets Mercury is closest to the sun.

If Inanna developed along the same line, then one can date the recognition of the identity of the evening star and the morning star before the rise, or together with the rise, of anthropomorphic deities in Babylonia.

Inanna is identified with the planet Venus in all historical periods. Yet she seems to have been venerated typically in her position as evening star. When Lugalbanda regains consciousness, after having been left alone and ill in the mountain wilderness between Uruk and Aratta, he turns to those gods whom he can reach out there.[16] First, he addresses the setting sun; second, Inanna; third, the moon; and finally, the rising sun. Inanna is obviously standing in the evening sky. She is there, too, as wife of Dumuzi, according to a passage from the hymn, "The lady of numerous powers:"[17]

> "As you, Inanna, hurry to the lap of your bridegroom Dumuzi,
> your seven bridesmen prepare the bed . . .
> When the star turns to . . . in the evening,
> when Utu enters the Ganun,
> while you, Inanna, inspire awe (standing) high, like a torch . . . "

The same general context is provided by the sacred marriage between Inanna and the king as Dumuzi incarnate. There, too, she is the evening star:[18]

> "The man cleans himself, the woman makes herself shining,
> the ox turns the head out of its yoke,

[12] P. Gössmann, *Planetarium Babylonicum* no. 383.
[13] A. Falkenstein, *ZA* 55 (1963) 33f.
[14] P. Gössmann, l.c. no. 260.
[15] "Calf" is a common element of male personal names in the earliest Sumerian onomasticon.
[16] C. Wilcke, *Das Lugalbanda-epos*, 81.
[17] *BE* 31, 12 rs. 18ff. = UM 55-21-368 III 15ff.
[18] Lines 90-98 and 115-116.

the sheep in their pen crowd the ground,
the numerous bucks and donkeys of Shakan, the living things of the steppe,
the four-legged creatures under the wide sky,
in garden, meadow, and green marsh,
the fishes in the water and the birds in the sky,
go to their rest.
The living beings, the numerous people bend their knees before my lady.
Those who lie on the roof, those who lie on the wall
. . . bring their worries before her."

2. Ishtar

The goddess Ishtar is a composite deity, partly Semitic and partly Sumerian. When the Akkadians settled in northern Babylonia, they assimilated the culture of the alluvium, which was at that time predominantly Sumerian. Sumerians and Akkadians were different peoples, with different backgrounds, but a similar religion—anthropomorphic polytheism. Among the gods of both peoples were forces of nature which had been individualized, among them, celestial bodies. The specific anthropomorphic characteristics were, however, often quite different. For the Sumerians the sun was a young man; for Semites, and among them the pre-Babylonian Akkadians, it was a woman. When Sumerians and Akkadians met, they did not argue about the number of suns, they must have argued about the sex of the sun. The result of the argument we know. The Akkadians took over the indigenous concept. The same process occurred in the case of the Venus deity, as S. Moscati has stated very clearly:[19] "A me sembra che, con processo analogo se inverso a quello che avviene per Shamash, si possa qui supporre un carattere originariamente maschile della divinità, il quale muta poi in Mesopotamia sotto l'influsso della corrispondente dea sumerica Inanna." Moscati's statement implies the existence of a Venus deity among Sumerians and Akkadians at the time they met. We have already seen that this can be confirmed for the Sumerians. If confirmation is deemed necessary for the Akkadians, it is much harder to get. The pre-Babylonian Akkadians are a prehistoric people without sources for their beliefs about Ishtar. Yet a deity of that name occurs among the inland Syrians of around 2500 B.C. in Ebla (Ashtar); the coastal Syrians of the Late Bronze Age (around 1300 B.C.) in Ugarit (ʿṯtr); the southern Canaanites of the 9th century B.C., in Moab (ʿštr); the Arabs of the 7th century B.C. near Assyria (A-tar); and the Arabs in the ancient kingdoms of Yemen in the first millennium B.C. and the first half of the first millennium A.D. (ʿṯtr). It so happens that there is proof for the planetary aspect of this pan-Semitic deity only in the case of the southern Arabian ʿṯtr. So far, even this proof stands on a slim foundation. J. Plessis assessed the situation correctly when he wrote: "il faut remarquer cependant que l'identification d'Attar avec la planète Venus est simplement probable, les documents de l'Arabie du Sud n'en fournissant

[19] *Studi Semitici* I (1958) 125.

pas de preuve décisive."[20] The probability was derived from a comparison with the Babylonian Ishtar, a derivation which is useless for our argument because we want to confirm the planetary aspect of the pre-Babylonian Ishtar. Since Plessis made his statement, decisive confirmation of the planetary aspect of the southern Arabian ʿṯtr is contained in the double epithet šrqn wġrbn, "the eastern and western one."[21]

The planetary aspect of the Ugaritic ʿṯtr is so far not attested. One expects it, of course, and some have tried to force information to that effect at any cost out of the mythological texts from Ugarit. A statement of M. Dahood may serve as example: "The astral nature of Aṯtar may also be inferred from Ugarit text 5:1 where the verb ʿrb is used of the goddess ʿṯtrt: kʿtrb ʿṯtrt 'when Attart sets'."[22] ʿṯtr and ʿṯtrt are two separate deities, as Herrmann felt necessary to state,[23] and moreover, tʿrb [sic] means simply "entered" as the context here and in a new text shows.[24] A. Caquot goes to the other extreme when he concludes ex silentio that ʿṯtr had no astral aspect whatsoever.[25]

The Eblaite Ashtar brings us back to the point where we started. In a list of pairs of gods consisting of an Eblaite and a corresponding Babylonian deity, Ashtar is paired with Ishtar.[26] The tertium comparationis cannot have been the anthropomorphic aspect of these deities because Ashtar is male and Ishtar is female. If it is non-anthropomorphic, it is most likely the representation of the planet Venus.

The change of sex from Ashtar to Ishtar was complete, but residues of the male deity survived in Babylonia. Halfway between Ebla and Babylonia, in Mari, both deities, the male Syrian Ashtar and the female Babylonian Ishtar were venerated side by side. The former is called here, "male Ishtar,"[27] the latter, simply "Ishtar." In northern Babylonia and Assyria the male gender survives as an aspect of the goddess. In an astrological text from the library of Assurbanipal, a sequence of omens derived from the appearance of Venus in the course of various months is interrupted by an explanatory section.[28] Venus, here called Dilbad, is characterized according to its position as evening star and morning star. The former is called female and identified with Ishtar of Uruk, the latter is called male and identified with Ishtar of Akkad. In a bilingual hymn from 8th century Assyria, the goddess Nanay identifies

[20] Étude sur les textes concernant Ištar-Astarté, 144[2].
[21] A. Jamme, *Le Muséon* 60 (1947) 88.
[22] *Studi Semitici* I (1958) 85f.
[23] W. Herrmann, *MIO* 15 (1969) 25[51].
[24] *Ugaritica* V 582 no. 9, 18.
[25] A. Caquot, *Syria* 35 (1958) 45-60.
[26] Excerpts from this list were discussed by G. Pettinato, in Chicago, (October 1977) and communicated to me by B. Knapp. The equation is between aš-dar and dINANNA. The latter can be read dinanna or dištar. The reading dištar is more likely because the same text equates zu-i-nu with dEN.ZU, that is the Akkadian variety of the Babylonian moon god. Ištar is written dINANNA at this period in Mari. Only when the name is part of a personal name is it written $eš_4$-tár. This latter spelling suggests that the name was pronounced Eštar, or even Aštar, in Mari and elsewhere in Babylonia at this time. With "Ištar" we designate in the following the Akkadian Venus deity, regardless of possible different pronunciations throughout Babylonian history.
[27] J. Bottéro, *Studi Semitici* I (1958) 41. D.O. Edzard, XV *RAI* 54, leaves the reading of dINANNA.UŠ open.
[28] K 5990, C. Virolleaud, *Istar* VIII.

herself with goddesses from various Assyrian and Babylonian cities, among them the "hierodule, Ishtar of Uruk" and the "male," respectively "bearded Ishtar of Babylon."[29] In a prayer of Assurbanipal the otherwise clearly female Ishtar of Ninive wears a beard.[30]

The first two texts give the impression that Ishtar of Akkad and Ishtar of Babylon were male. There is overwhelming evidence from numerous sources that both are female. The answer for the divergence lies in the connection of the northern Ishtar with the morning star, and the southern Ishtar with the evening star. We have seen that the southern Ishtar, that is, Inanna of Uruk, was typically venerated as the evening star. The connection of the northern Ishtar with the morning star becomes understandable when we are aware that the Semitic Venus deities were typically venerated as the morning star.[31] The same concept may also stand behind the description of Ishtar of Ninive in Assurbanipal's prayer. The fact that she is female and wears a beard does not describe an androgynous monster. Ishtar wears the beard only when she stands in the morning sky. We can, therefore, not really make a case for the androgynous nature of Ishtar, and have to abstain from using this alleged androgyny for strengthening the weak case of 'ṯtr's androgyny in Syria and southern Arabia.[32] However, within the planetary aspect Ishtar did change sex, a concept which may have spread. The Hurrian deity Shaushka, for example, was identified with Ishtar and appears as god and goddess in the rock carvings of Yazilikaya.[33] Further, a clearly bisexual deity, Aphroditos, was venerated in Amathus on Cyprus, a settlement with eastern connections. Aphroditos was female, but wore a beard. In ceremonies given in its honour, women were required to wear men's clothes, and vice versa.[34]

3. Nanay

E. Reiner has published a self-laudatory hymn of Nanay which is dated 744 or 734 B.C.[35] In it Nanay claims identity with a number of Mesopotamian goddesses, among them, Ishtar. The planetary aspect of Ishtar is expressly mentioned as a point in the equation. We have to conclude that Nanay was a Venus deity at that time. Some 1,750 years later, the Syrian lexicographer Bar Bahlul mentions Nanay in his Syriac-Arabic dictionary as name for Venus among "the Arabs." Already the oldest phases in the documentation of the history of this goddess[36] contain indications that Nanay was a Venus deity all along. During the Ur III

[29] E. Reiner, *JNES* 33 (1975) 221-236.

[30] K 1286, 6 = *ABRT* I 7.

[31] See below, under Aziz and Uzza.

[32] Cf. for example M. Höfner, *WM* I 498.

[33] Cf. *WM* I, Kleinasien, s.v. Ištar.

[34] *RE*, s.v. Aphroditos and Aphrodite, p. 2760 no. 16.

[35] See above, note 29.

[36] Ur III period: documents from Puzrishdagan mention offerings to Nanay of Uruk (An. Or. 19, no. 316); documents from Ur record quantities of precious metals used for the manufacture of Nanay-statuettes (*UET* III, nos. 509, 525, 529, 538, 740).

Isin-Larsa period: composition of a hymn to Nanay mentioning Isbi-Erra (2017-1985) (W. Hallo, *BiOr*. 23 [1966] 242ff.).

Early Old Babylonian period: the year date Sumula'el 26 (1972) records the erection of statues of Nanay and Inanna in Babylon (*RLA* Datenlisten); construction of the Ehegala for Nanay in Uruk by

period she was venerated in Uruk, the city of Inanna. Offerings were made to her jointly with Inanna and An in Uruk, in the Early Old Babylonian period. This suggests that she shared quarters with Inanna and An, in the E'ana of Uruk. Her shrine within the E'ana is called Ehegala under Sinkashid, Eme'urur under Singamil and Anam, Eshahula under Rimsin, and Ehili'ana in the Kassite and Neo-Assyrian periods. The name Eme'urur still appears in a Neo-Babylonian festival calendar.[37] When Hammurapi built the Eturkalama in Babylon, An, Inanna, and Nanay were housed in this temple which thus became virtually a replica of the E'ana.

Nanay was also venerated in Kish during the Late Old Babylonian period. Since Kish was also one of the centers of the cult of Inanna, one suspects that there, too, Nanay was venerated side by side with Inanna. The fact that Nanay shares the temple of Inanna in Uruk and Babylon becomes significant when we look at the nature of Nanay and her

Sinkashid (1865-35); construction of the Eme'urur for Nanay in Uruk by Singamil (1834-22); completion of the Eme'urur for Nanay by Anam (1821-17); documents from the time of Anam mention offerings received jointly by An, Inanna, and Nanay (A. Falkenstein, *BaM* 2 [1963] 32ff.); construction of the Eshahula for Nanay in Uruk (?) by Kudurmabuk and Rimsin (between 1817 and 1763) (*SAK* 220f.); appearance of PNN mentioning Nanay in documents dated to the reign of Rimsin (*UET* V, no. 304); construction of the temple Eturkalama for An, Inanna, and Nanay in Babylon, according to the year date Hammurapi 34 (1785) (*RLA* Datenlisten and A. Falkenstein, l.c. 32); composition of a hymn to Nanay mentioning Samsu'iluna (1749-12) (*VS* X 215).

Late Old Babylonian period: priests (sanga and ērib bīti) of Nanay appear as witnesses in documents from Kish (*YOS* XIII, cf. index s.v. Nana); a street in this city is called "Nanay-street" (*YOS* XIII, no. 192).

Kassite period: construction of the shrine Ehili'ana within the temple E'ana in Uruk by Nazimaruttash (1345-24) (*YOS* I 40, 12); guarantee by Nanay for a land donation of Melishipak (1188-74) to the princess Hunnubat-Nanay (*MDP* X 87ff.).

Neo-Assyrian period: in 849, Shalmaneser III offers to the principal gods of Babylonia including Nanay, "lady of Babylon" (Balawat inscription VI 2-3); restoration of the Ehili'ana in Uruk by Eriba-Marduk (783-62) (*YOS* I 40, 13); donation of offerings for Nanay and Marbiti of the Ezida in Borsippa to priests of Nabu, Nanay, Marbiti, and Sutitu from the 8th year of Nabushumishkun (before 743) (*RA* 16 [1919] 141ff.); copy of a self-laudatory hymn to Nanay, from Assyria, dated to 744 or 734 (E. Reiner, *JNES* 33 [1975] 221ff.); removal of the statues of Inanna and Nanay from the E'ana in Uruk by Assyrian troops (700) *I R* 43, 41); rebuilding of the Ehili'ana by Essarhadon (after 680) (*YOS* I 40 and *RA* 11 [1914] 96); recovery of a statue of Nanay by Assurbanipal in Elam, and its installation in the Ehili'ana (*Rassam cyl.* VI 107ff.).

Neo-Babylonian period: reinstallation of the statues of Nabu and Nanay in the Ezida of Borsippa by Nebukadnezar II (604-562) (*NBK* 92 II 18f); reinstallation of the statue of Nanay in Uruk by the same ruler (l.c. 51f.).

Seleucid period: one of the kings named Antiochus is murdered by priests in a temple of Nanay somewhere in Mesopotamia (2 *Macc* 1, 13ff.).

Parthian period: Nanay is venerated in Palmyra, Dura (under the name Artemis), Hatra, Assur, Susa, and eastern Iran (G. Azarpay, *JAOS* 96 [1976] 537f.).

Sassanian period: together with Shamesh, Sin, and Bel, Nanay is invoked in an incantation found at Nippur (J. Montgomery, *Aramaic incantation texts from Nippur*, 238). Jacob of Sarug (521 A.D.) mentions Nanay as goddess of the Assyrians (S. Landerdorfer, *MVAG* 21 [1916] 110ff.). "Assyrians" are the inhabitants of the Sassanian province Adiabene which, incidentally, is geographically the heart-land of Ancient Assyria.

Islamic period: Bar Bahlul (circa 1000 A.D.) mentions Nanay as name of Venus among the "Arabs" (cf. below, note 54).

[37] *SBH* VII and *BRM* IV 25.

theologic relationship to Inanna. According to the hymn of Ishbi-Erra, Inanna delegated some of her powers to Nanay: "Nanay, ornament of the E'ana, created for the hierodule (Inanna)"; "summoned as queen of all the lands by the hierodule Inanna"; "luxurious attributes have been generously given to you by the hierodule Inanna."[38] A comparison of the hymn of Ammiditana to Ishtar[39] and of Samsu'iluna to Nanay, yields terminological similarities between the two deities in the sector conventionally labelled "love." Both deities are said to possess mašrahu, kuzbu, ru'āmu, and bāštu.[40] Nanay shares also the aspect "war" with Ishtar. In the text recording a donation, from the time of Nabu-shumishkun, Nanay is called qarittu, "heroine." In the same text, she is also called "sister of Shamash," as is Ishtar elsewhere. The hymn of Ishbi-Erra contains further "astral" characterizations, which indicate that she shared the planetary aspect with Inanna and Ishtar. She "emerges brightly like the daylight" and is "a woman being verily a heavenly star."[41]

By the Neo-Assyrian period it becomes clear that Nanay has become an important deity, and emancipated from the shadow of Inanna. We have already mentioned the self-laudatory hymn where she claims identity with Ishtar and other goddesses. One hundred years earlier, Shalmaneser III counts her among the principal deities of Babylonia, and calls her "lady of Babylon." Her veneration has spread to Borsippa where she becomes the wife of Nabu. She survives the end of the Neo-Babylonian empire. Her cult spreads far–from Palmyra to Transoxiana–as G. Azarpay has demonstrated. It is obvious that the history of Nanay and that of the Arameans exhibit parallels. Nanay gains power when the Arameans constitute a significant segment of Babylonian population. Later, her cult spreads together with Aramean culture. She may even have been Aramean all along. This theory would explain the form of her name,[42] and also her curious relationship with Inanna. In Uruk, and later in Babylon, she shares a temple with Inanna, respectively, Ishtar. Why should there be two Venus deities in one temple? One may feel tempted to assume that the constituency of both deities was ethnically different. The Sumerians were Inanna's constituency. Could not the Arameans have been that of Nanay? It is, of course, difficult to believe that Arameans could have lived in southern Babylonia 600 years before they are attested as Ahlamu in northern Mesopotamia. On the other hand, the Sumerians may well have had Semitic nomads as western neighbours who were partly Arameans. Some of these would have settled down in southern Babylonia without leaving much of a trace, because they assimilated the alluvial culture.

[38] W. Hallo, *BiOr*. 23 (1966) 242ff., lines 2, 3, and 24.

[39] *RA* 22 (1925) 169ff.

[40] Approximate meanings: "fullness (of flesh)," "charm," "loving," "?."

[41] Hallo, l.c. lines 1 and 7.

[42] The name Nanay is not Akkadian or Sumerian. It does not seem to be Amorite either. It is spelled ^{d}na-na-a, or ^{d}na-na-a-a. The former spelling is more common and represents the basis for the conventional transcription Nanâ. The latter spelling indicates, however, that the pronunciation was Nanay, or Nanaya. The Greek transcription is nanaia, Aramaic nny, or nn'y. Nanay could well be an Aramaic name where -ay is an old feminine ending (T. Nöldecke, *Syrische Grammatik* 83). The etymologies of Zimmern, deLagarde, and Hoffmann (cf. Février, *La réligion des Palmyréniens* [1931] 99^{2}) are far-fetched.

4. Aziz and Uzza

The god Aziz is known from inscriptions found in Palmyra and the Roman province Dacia–and from the speech of Julian, the Apostate, to Helios. His planetary character is proven by ex-voto inscriptions from Dacia in Latin, dedications of Syrians who took part in the resettlement of the war-ravaged country when it was made a Roman province in A.D. 107. In only one of these inscriptions is the god called by his name: *deo Azizo bono p[uero . . .]*.[43] In the others, the *deus bonus puer* [. . .] is called Phosphorus, "morning star."[44] One has drawn the conclusion that Aziz was a morning star deity and not a Venus deity.[45] Such an interpretation led necessarily to a search for a corresponding evening star deity which was believed to be found in a passage from Julian: "The inhabitants of Emesa, a place from time immemorial sacred to Helios, associate with Helios in their temples Monimos and Azizos. Iamblichus . . . says that the secret meaning to be interpreted is that Monimos is Hermes and Azizos is Ares, the assessors of Helios who are the channel for many blessings to the region of our earth."[46] Here, however, Monimos seems to be Mercury (= Hermes) and not the evening star. Azizos as Venus, and Monimos as Mercury, would make plausible assessors of Helios inasmuch as they are the two inner planets which are always seen close to the sun. Yet can we really identify Azizos with Venus, in the light of the identification with Phosphorus in the inscriptions from Dacia? The identification of Arabic Venus deities with the morning star has parallels. Uzza is identified with Lucifer by Jerome (see below). Further, the South Arabian 'ṯtr is often described as šrqn, "the eastern one," and Ishtar of northern Babylonia retains the morning star aspect when contrasted with Inanna of southern Babylonia (see above). One concludes that Aziz was a Venus deity which was venerated typically as the morning star.

In Palmyra, Aziz, here spelled 'zyzw, is paired with 'rṣw in the inscription CIS II 3974, which has been treated repeatedly.[47] The inscription is found below a relief on which can be seen two gods: one on horseback, the other riding a camel. The horseman is Aziz, according to a second relief depicting the god on horseback. The inscription mentions 'zyzw.[48] He is not a child, as the inscriptions from Dacia indicate, but a young warrior, which recalls Iamblichos' identification with Ares. Like Monimos, 'rṣw is conventionally connected with the evening star, because he occurs together with Aziz, the alleged morning star.[49]

[43] *CIL* III 875.

[44] *CIL* III 1130ff.

[45] *WM* I 428 s.v. Azizos.

[46] Quoted from the Loeb Classical Library, *The works of Emperor Julian* (1913) *Or* IV 150C. The mss. have Edessa which Spanheim (*Juliani opera* [1696]) emended to Emesa in accordance with the fame of the sun cult in that city. Cf. also J.B. Segal, *Edessa, the blessed city*, (1970) 106[1].

[47] Sobernheim, *Palmyrenische Inschriften BA* 4 (1899-1902) 211ff.; *CIS* II 3974 (with earlier literature); J.T. Milik, *Dédicaces faites par des dieux*, *Bibliothèque archéologique et historique XCII* (1972), 22f.

[48] J.T. Milik, l.c.

[49] *WM* I 463.

Aziz is an Arabic deity, as J. G. Février concludes from the Palmyrene spelling of his name.[50] The name is an adjective which originally should have been used to qualify a god with a different name. This god should be a Venus deity like Aziz, that is, ‘ṯtr. Indeed, the southern Arabian ‘ṯtr is qualified by ‘zz in two Sabean inscriptions, one from the first century B.C., and the other from the first century A.D.[51]

The Arabic feminine elative of ‘azīz with the definite article is al-‘Uzza, the name of a goddess whose veneration flourished in Arabia just before the rise of Islam. The goddess and her cult have been treated extensively by J. Wellhausen in 1897 and by T. Fahd in 1968.[52] In sources from the fifth century A.D., she is identified with Aphrodite by an anonymous Syrian historian; with Kaukabta, "the female star;" with Balthi, by Isaac of Antioch; and finally with Lucifer, the morning star, by Jerome.[53] This last identification is of particular importance for our topic because it indicates that al-‘Uzza was venerated as the morning star ("*colunt autem illam ob Luciferam cuius cultui Saracenorum natio dedita est*"). Around 1000 A.D. the Syrian lexicographer, Bar Bahlul, lists ‘wzy as the name of Venus among the Ṭayy, a powerful Arabic tribe.[54] Al-Uzza may also have been identical with ‘Azuz, a goddess whose cult in Harran was destroyed by the Romans, according to An-Nadim,[55] a contemporary of Bar Bahlul.

As Venus deity who was venerated as the morning star, and whose name is derived from the root ‘zz, al-‘Uzza must have been connected with Aziz. One may explain the difference in sex according to the Babylonian example of Ishtar and Inanna: when the Arabs came under Aramean influence on the northern borders of their territory, they adopted the female sex of Venus from the Arameans who called her Kaukabta, Balthi, or Nanay. However, we know of a deity with the name ‘zy in southern Arabia.[56] Subjects of Šaʻir Awtar (circa 65-55 B.C.)[57] king of Saba and Ḏū-Raidan, dedicate a horse and a golden image to ‘zyn.[58] While ‘zyn is female here, it is male in one inscription from Qataban.[59] Nothing is known about his or her nature. M. Höfner pointed out that ‘zyn is linguistically the exact South Arabic counterpart of Arabic al-‘Uzza. She goes on to state that the northern al-‘Uzza moved south where she became ‘zyn.[60] It would be easier to assume

[50] Février, *La réligion des Palmyréniens* 16[5].

[51] A. Jamme, *Sabaean inscriptions from Mahram Bilqis* (1962), Ja 559, 18f. and 631, 20. A further example for the connection of a Venus deity with qualifying ‘zz comes from an Aramean incantation bowl (J.A. Montgomery, l.c. no. 28): dlybt ‘zyzt' = dlīḇaṯ ‘zīztā. Dlīḇaṯ is, of course, the Sumerian Venus-name Dilbat, which occurs also in Bar Bahlul as name for Venus in Babel (R. Duval, l.c.).

[52] *Reste arabischen Heidentums* 34-45; *Le Panthéon de l'Arabie centrale a la veille de l'Hégire*, *Bibl. arch. et hist.* XXXVIII (1968) 163-182.

[53] Wellhausen, l.c.

[54] Cf. R. Duval, *Lexicon Syriacum Auctore Hassano, Bar Bahlule* (1901) I 244f. Bar Bahlul differentiates between Arbaye and Ṭayyaye. Arbaye is a translation of Arabic ‘arab. The latter term designates specifically the settled Arabs, while 'A‘rab designates the nomadic Arabs. (cf. Lisān al-‘Arab s.v. ‘rb). The nomads are called Ṭayyaye after the powerful trible of that name. The name Nanay, which was in use among the settled Arabs, represents an Aramaic survival; the name of Venus among the nomads represents a survival of al-‘Uzzā.

[55] D. Chwolson, *Die Ssabier und der Ssabismus* II (1856) 34.

[56] *WM* I 548 s.v. ‘Uzzayan.

[57] A. Jamme, *Sabaean Inscr.* . . . 390f.

[58] *RES* 4149. The /n/ in ‘zyn is the definite article.

[59] A. Jamme, *Quatre inscriptions sud-arabes*, 1957.

[60] *WM* I 548.

the opposite, because 'zyn is attested earlier in the south. Southern origin is still indicated by Bar Bahlul's attribution of 'wzy to the Ṭayy.

5. Balthi

In his two poems about the desctruction of Bet Hur, Isaac of Antioch gives an example for the futility and the danger inherent in paganism, expecially in the worship of Venus, who is called here Kaukabta, "the (female) star."[60a] He points out that the pagan Beduin women are not more beautiful than other women though they make offerings to Venus and ask her for attractiveness. He argues further that the worship of Venus has not saved the inhabitants of Bet Hur from being sacked by the Beduins, who worship Venus just as they do. Isaac calls the Venus of the Beduins 'wzy, and the Venus of Bet Hur, Balthi. It is not possible to document the history of Balthi before the 5th century A.D. In sources from Palmyra, a goddess blty appears together with bl.[61] This connection makes it unlikely that blty is Balthi, because bl is the Babylonian Bel, i.e., Marduk, whose consort is Ṣarpanītu,and not the Venus deity Ištar or Nanay. It is also unclear who is meant in the Latin dedication to "*Balti diae divinae*" from Aquincum.[62] Even among Syriac writers, Balthi is not always the same goddess. Meliton, the philosopher, calls the city goddess of Byblos, Balthi.[63]

Balthi, the Venus deity of Bet Hur, can hardly be al-'Uzza because that goddess is attributed to the Beduins of the time. She is, rather, of ancient Mesopotamian origin, as Bar Bahlul suggests when he lists blty as the name for Venus among the Chaldeans. Indeed, the pagan gods of the Oshroene, where Bet Hur was in all likelihood located,[64] are clearly of Babylonian origin: Nabu and Bel are the principal gods of the pagans in Edessa.[65] Sin, Nabu, and Bel were still venerated in early Islamic times in Harran.[66] Balthi was venerated here too, and some peculiarities of her nature and cult are preserved in Arabic accounts of the religion of the Sabeans of Harran.[67] If we accept her Babylonian origin, we can understand the name as derived from Akkadian bēlti, "my lady," which should have been originally an epithet of Ištar or Nanay.

6. Astarte

Astarte is usually understood to be the Canaanite counterpart of Ištar. This is contradicted by the evidence from Ebla from around 2500 B.C., where Ištar is identified with Aštar, and not with the Eblaite Aštarta. It is confirmed, on the other hand, by the

[60a] Isaac Antiochenus, ed. Bickell I 210ff.

[61] J.G. Février, *La réligion* . . . 64f.

[62] *CIL* III Suppl. 10393.

[63] W. Cureton, *Spicilegium Syriacum* (1855) 44; cf. the Syriac text on page kh.

[64] Exact location not known. The other cities mentioned by Isaac are located in the Oshroene, i.e., Edessa itself, Harran and Nisibis.

[65] Cf. the account of the martyrdom of Sharbil in W. Cureton, *Ancient Syriac Documents* (1864) 41, lines 20ff.

[66] Cf. D. Chwolson, l.c. II in the index.

[67] D. Chwolson, l.c. II 23, 33f. 40.

evidence from Ugarit, of the 14th century B.C., where Ištar appears in the place of ʿṯtrt in parallel lists of Babylonian and Ugaritic gods.[68] Indeed, the two deities have much in common:

1. the aspect of "war"– For Astarte this aspect is best documented in Egyptian sources from the New Kingdom. It is also indicated in Ugaritic sources which connect ʿṯtrt to horses, the use of which was the major development in the art of warfare during that period. She is also mentioned in a curse which attests her competence in killing: "May Horon break your head, " ʿṯtrt-šm-bʿl your skull."[69]

2. the aspect of "love"– The evidence for Astarte as a goddess of love is meager. Like ʿAnat, she is an image of beauty in Ugarit. Yet this may merely mean that she was beautiful as befits any young goddess. According to Jeremia, the "queen of heaven," who is Astarte, as we shall see presently, was worshipped typically by women.[70] It may mean that she was a mother-goddess, to whom the women turned in their labour, and in the care for the infant. It may mean that she was a love-goddess, to whom they turned for beauty and fertility. Confirmation for the latter comes from the ancient Greeks. Aphrodite is doubtlessly a goddess of love, and she was believed to have come to Greece from the east, particularly from Cyprus, and, according to Herodot, from Askelon.[71] Modern scholars concur, and even hold it likely that the name Aphrodite is derived from Astarte.[72] If Aphrodite is Astarte in Greece, one cannot brush aside the aspect of a love-goddess as interpretatio graeca, as W. Herrmann suggests.[73]

3. the aspect of rulership over the heaven–Again, the main sources for this aspect of Astarte are Egyptian, where the goddess is called "lady of heaven." [74] The same aspect underlies Herodotus' designation of Astarte of Askelon as "Aphrodite Urania." That the latter was, in fact, Astarte is confirmed by an inscription from Delos, dated after 160 B.C., which was authored by a citizen of Askelon and addressed to "Aphrodite Urania, Astarte Palaistine."[75] Also, the "queen of heaven," whom Jeremia mentions, was in all probability Astarte, and not Istar, as seems to be the current opinion. That opinion is based on the belief that the "queen of heaven" is one member of the "host of heaven" and that the latter refers to Mesopotamian astral deities. I do not find the arguments which have been advanced to strengthen this theory at all compelling,[76] and believe that it is very unlikely that the Assyrians, or the Babylonians, exported their deities together with their rule. Assur, Marduk, and Nabu, by far the most important Mesopotamian deities, never left the borders of Mesopotamia. Ištar, in particular, was not even worshipped among the Canaanites, or the Arameans, outside of Mesopotamia.

[68] *Ugaritica* V 44f.
[69] W. Herrmann, *MIO* 15 (1969) 19ff.
[70] VII 18.
[71] *Herodotus* I 105.
[72] W. Herrmann, l.c. 40.
[73] W. Herrmann, l.c. 41ff.
[74] *ANET*, 3rd edition with suppl. 250.
[75] F. Durrbach, *Inscriptions de Délos* (1937) no. 2305.
[76] A survey of these arguments can be found in J. Plessis, *Étude* . . . 202ff.; additional arguments in M. Weinfeld, *Ugarit-Forschungen* IV (1972) 133-154. The latter seems to admit that there are enough Canaanite astral deities to constitute a "host of heaven" when he says (p. 150): "Ultimately Baal is also called Baalshamem, and he cannot therefore be entirely dissociated from the worship of the 'host of heaven.' Nor can Ashera be separated from Ashtoret and Anat, both of whom are called 'the queen of heaven.'"

How should she have come to Juda? On the other hand, Canaanite deities appear as pagan substrat in the area of ancient Hebrew monotheism. The "queen of heaven" was surely a Canaanite deity; in all probability, Astarte, the "lady of heaven" of Merneptah, the "heavenly" Aphrodite of Herodotus.

The aspects of war, love, and rulership over the heaven may not have constituted the entire tertium comparationis between Istar and Astarte. Yet they alone must have made the equation possible. We do not have to assume that Istar's planetary aspect was part of it. On the contrary, there are indications that Astarte had no planetary aspect:

1. there is reason to believe that 'ṯtr was the Venus deity of Ugarit;

2. if Astarte was a Venus deity, one would expect that Aphrodite was also a Venus deity. This is true only for the time after Aristotle. Originally, Aphrodite was not connected with Venus. Long after that connection, the planetary aspect of Aphrodite was transferred to Astarte, her Phoenician counterpart. It is documented by Byzantine writers like Lydos, and the lexicographer, Suidas.[77]

7. Summary

The Sumerians and all well-documented ancient Semitic peoples possessed a Venus deity. The recognition of the identity of the evening star with the morning star is prehistoric and precedes the fusion of the planetary and the anthropomorphic aspects of the Venus deities. The Sumerian Venus deity is female, Semitic Venus deities outside Mesopotamia are as a rule male. The originally male Akkadian Venus deity Ištar changed sex under Sumerian influence. The northern Arabian Venus deity al-'Uzza is female. She supersedes in northern Arabia the male Venus deity Aziz. The change in sex from Aziz to al-'Uzza may be due to the Aramean Venus deity (Nanay, Balthi, Kaukabta). It is possible, however, that al-'Uzza stems from southern Arabia where she would have been far removed from Aramean influence.

The opinion that the Canaanites and the northern Arabians possessed separate deities representing the morning star and the evening star cannot be upheld. Astarte was not linked with Venus or the evening star prior to the Byzantine period. The northern Arabian Monimos was not identified with the evening star but with Mercury. It is not known whether Arṣu had a planetary aspect at all and he cannot be linked with the evening star in particular.

The Venus deities al-'Uzza, Aziz, the southern Arabian 'ṯtr, and probably also the Ugaritic 'ṯtr, the Eblaite Aštar and the original Akkadian Ištar were venerated as the morning star; the Sumerian Venus deity, Inanna, as evening star. The fusion of Inanna and Ištar in Babylonia produced a Babylonian Venus deity which was male and northern Babylonian as the morning star and female and southern Babylonian as the evening star.

He also notes that the ceremonies held on roof tops for the "host of heaven" in general, and the "queen of heaven" in particular, are not only found in Assyria, but also among the Hittites. Indeed, what is more appropriate than worshipping celestial deities from a place where one can see them best?

[77] Cf. *RE* s.v. Astarte.

SOURCES AND MONOGRAPHS ON THE ANCIENT NEAR EAST

Editors: Giorgio Buccellati, Marilyn Kelly-Buccellati

These two series make available original documents in English translation (Sources) and important studies by modern scholars (Monographs) as a contribution to the study of history, religion, literature, art and archaeology of the Ancient Near East. Inexpensive and flexible in format, they are meant to serve the specialist by bringing within easy reach basic publications often in updated versions, to provide imaginative educational outlets for undergraduate and graduate courses, and to reach the interested segments of the educated lay audience.

SOURCES FROM THE ANCIENT NEAR EAST

Volume One

Fasicle 1: R. I. Caplice, *The Akkadian Namburbi Texts: An Introduction.* 24 pp.

Fascicle 2: M. E. Cohen, *Balag-Compositions: Sumerian Lamentation Liturgies of the Second and First Millennium B.C.* 34 pp.

Fascicle 3: Luigi Cagni, *The Poem of Erra.* 62 pp.

Fascicle 4: Gary Beckman, *Hittite Birth Rituals: An Introduction.* 21 pp.

Fascicle 5: S. M. Burstein, *The* Babyloniaca *of Berossus.* 39 pp.

MONOGRAPHS ON THE ANCIENT NEAR EAST

Volume One

Fascicle 1: A. Falkenstein, *The Sumerian Temple City* (1954). Introduction and Translation by M. deJ. Ellis. 21 pp.

Fascicle 2: B. Landsberger, *Three Essays on the Sumerians* (1943-1945). Introduction and Translation by M. deJ. Ellis. 18 pp.

Fascicle 3: I. M. Diakonoff, *Structure of Society and State in Early Dynastic Sumer* (1959). Summary and Translation of selected passages by the author. Introduction by M. Desrochers. 16 pp.

Fascicle 4: B. Landsberger, *The Conceptual Autonomy of the Babylonian World* (1926). Translation by Th. Jacobsen, B. Foster and H. von Siebenthal. Introduction by Th. Jacobsen. 16 pp.

Fascicle 5: M. Liverani, *Three Amarna Essays* (1965-1972). Translation and Introduction by M. L. Jaffe. 34 pp.

Fascicle 6: P. Matthiae, *Ebla in the Period of the Amorite Dynasties* (1975). Translation and Introduction by M. L. Jaffe. 36 pp., 20 plates

Fascicle 7: G. Pettinato, *Old Canaanite Texts from Ebla* (1975). Translation and Introduction by M. L. Jaffe. 17 pp.

Volume Two

Fascicle 1: C. Saporetti, *The Status of Women in the Middle Assyrian Period.* Translation and Introduction by B. Boltze-Jordan. 20 pp.

Fascicle 2: N. Yoffee, *Explaining Trade in Ancient Western Asia.* 40 pp.

JNES STYLE SHEET
UNDENA PUBLICATIONS

General Procedures

A primary goal of Undena Publications is to publish at the lowest cost possible while keeping the highest possible standards. In order to do this we need your cooperation when submitting manuscripts. Please read the information below.

MANUSCRIPTS: Keep a duplicate copy of your submitted manuscript since this will not be included when proofs are sent to you.

PROOFS: Each author will receive proofs for corrections.

CORRECTIONS and CHANGES: Corrections and changes must be kept to an absolute minimum. Major changes, i.e. changes that affect more than a couple of lines, or a great many minor changes, will be at the author's expense, and subject to a $1.00 per change surcharge. All changes as submitted by the author on the proofs are suggestions only and may be disregarded at the discretion of the editor. Changes that affect entire pages will not be accepted.

COPIES: Besides 10 complimentary copies of the work, authors may take advantage of a one-time prepublication discount of 50% (plus postage and handling). Additional copies are available in unlimited quantity at 20% discount (plus postage and handling).

Manuscript Preparation

MANUSCRIPT: All material must be typed, double-spaced throughout on *non*-erasable and *non*-onionskin bond; photocopies are accepted. Isolated corrections may be entered by hand, but should be printed. The University of Chicago Press *Manual of Style* is recommended as a guide to style.

FOOTNOTES: All notes are to be typed, double-spaced, on separate pages with running numeration.

ABSTRACT: All manuscripts should be accompanied by an abstract of approximately 100-125 words.

TABLES and CHARTS: Tables and charts must be laid out as desired to appear in print, with explanations in the margin when the typed manuscript does not show clearly the intended format.

TITLES: Authors are strongly encouraged to divide their manuscripts into sections, subsections, etc., numbered and titled. There should be a table of contents (following the abstract) referring to these sections on the following model:

1. (Major heading)
    1.1. (Sub-heading)
    1.2. (Sub-heading)
        1.2.1. (Second level sub-heading)
        1.2.2. (Second level sub-heading)
2. (Major heading)

REFERENCES and BIBLIOGRAPHY: For all references please include (a) *Full* name of author(s), (b) place of publication *and* name of publisher, (c) page numbers of article.

UNDERSCORES:
Straight underline for *italics:*
Wavy underline for **bold face**:
Wavy and straight underline for ***bold italics***:
Double underline for SMALL CAPS:
Triple underline for REGULAR CAPS: